PAT ALBECK

QUEEN OF THE TEA TOWEL

First published in the United Kingdom in 2018 by National Trust Books
43 Great Ormond Street
London WCIN 3HZ

An imprint of Pavilion Books Group.

Photography by Jacqui Hurst, other than p.7 courtesy of Matthew Rice and p.8 courtesy of Alun Callender Photography.

ISBN: 9781911358466

A CIP catalogue record for this book is available from the British Library.

10 9 8 7 6 5 4 3 2 1

Reproduction by Mission, Hong Kong
Printed by G. Canale & C. SpA, Italy

This book can be ordered direct from the publisher at the website: www.pavilionbooks.com, or try your local bookshop.

Also available at National Trust shops or www.shop.nationaltrust.org.uk.

PAT ALBECK

QUEEN OF THE TEA TOWEL

Introduction by Matthew Rice

National Trust

PAT'S TEA TOWELS

Just as the programme serves as souvenir of a play, a lasting memory of the
visit to the theatre, so, for many years, the tea towel was a vital part of a visit
to a National Trust property. Millions of linen cloths were sold in Trust shops
nationwide and taken home. Many were pinned or hung on the kitchen wall, a
reminder of each of the pieces that make up the richest collection of property
ever amassed in the country.

By far the majority of these were designed by one woman whose background
– as the child of Jewish immigrants from Russian Poland – was as far from the
patrician ways of the twentieth-century National Trust as could be imagined. Pat
was the youngest daughter of Motel Albeck, a furrier. He and his wife Sarah had
arrived in London's East End in 1908 leaving behind their lives and families in the
shtetl of Zarimbe near Warsaw. They then moved to Hull, where Pat was born.

Motel, now renamed an anglicised Max, was quickly established in a new business
and sent the three eldest daughters to university. However with modest results
at School Certificate, Pat was quickly dispatched to the Hull School of Art where
she shone. Winning, in 1950, a place at the Royal College of Art, she left for
London. There she met her husband, Peter Rice, a painting student, and from
then on their lives were utterly devoted to design until their deaths in 2015 and
2017. At the RCA, Pat had studied in the textile school and worked in fashion
and furnishing design throughout the 1950s and '60s, but a chance meeting at a
dinner added a further dimension to her work.

Pat and Peter had moved from South Kensington (where they had settled
while at the RCA) to Chiswick Mall in 1963. In part the product of the intrusive
construction of the Great West Road the year before, this ribbon of variegated
houses was inadvertently isolated from the rest of grittier west London and

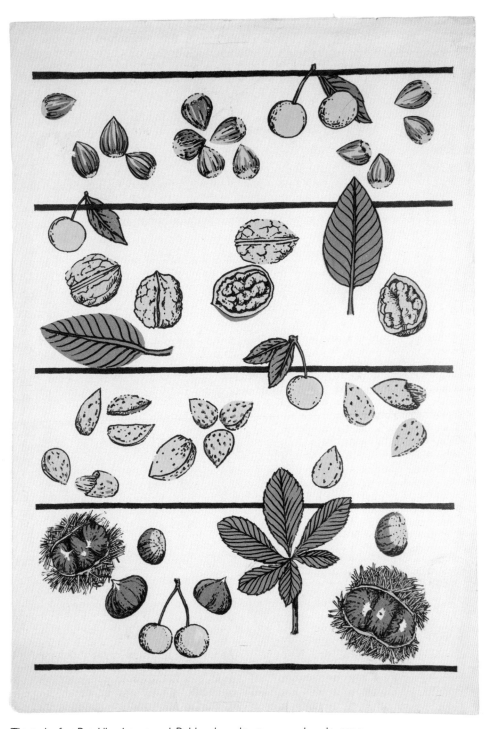

This is the first Pat Albeck tea towel. Bold and graphic, it was produced in 1954.

became an oasis of Thames-side quiet. It had already been established as an artistic enclave, and foremost amongst its residents at the time were the painters Mary Fedden and Julian Trevelyan. As close neighbours they instantly became friends of Pat and Peter. An introduction to Mary's cousin Robin, who was historic buildings officer at the Trust, led to a discussion about the possibility of Pat producing some 'illustrated dishcloths for the tables.' The tables were the low-key predecessors of the later ubiquitous National Trust shops, simply a table in the hall where some postcards were sold along with the property guidebooks. Pat was delighted and there began a fifty-year productive relationship.

If the tea towels defined Pat Albeck for many people it was conversely the case that her designs exemplified the extent and the tone of the Trust. Perhaps they even served in some way as a precursor to the more accessible and egalitarian organisation it was having so much difficulty in becoming. Pat's combination of informed acute observation and bold schematic design produced a representation of the houses, parks, kitchens and gardens of the Trust's estate that was itself a welcoming and familiar introduction to what had been the privilege of the few.

Pat designed over 300 tea towels for the Trust. This book is a record of that body of work, containing a selection of the designs that have given so much pleasure both to the members of the Trust and to their designer. Pat took her role seriously, with missionary zeal! Every design merited a visit to the place to be depicted, whether in Cornwall, Northumberland or Norfolk... Often in the company of her long-time commissioning editor Ray Hallet, she would inspect the property, working out exactly what constituted, for her, the most characteristic aspects of the place. Perhaps it was this approach that made her own observations chime so clearly with that of the visitors for whom she was designing. The Reformation, the Civil War, the Grand Tour or the Picturesque had little resonance for Pat, however the Industrial Revolution and the Arts

Pat at the Royal College of Art, 1951.

and Crafts movement meant rather more to a designer who came of age professionally in the post-Festival of Britain atmosphere of the 1950s when design seemed capable of changing the world.

Pat's perception of pattern and colour, her passion for gardens – more specifically for flowers – and her ability to see what was speaking to those who loved the places she illustrated made for a remarkable series of images. Briskly waving aside instructions from bristly, tweedy land agents or indeed former owners that 'the house is seen at its best from the south-east', Pat would assimilate details and elements that were seen as ancillary and unimportant to many but that proved to be just the telling detail that expressed the character of a place. Set-piece views of course made their appearances but their formality was frequently softened by a decorative border constructed of some more everyday or charming element: carrots, flower pots or teaspoons. Amongst her most popular designs are those that step outside the property-specific: wild flowers, butterflies, even cats of the National Trust became bestsellers and, in due course, collector's items.

Pat would begin with a rough design in miniature for discussion with what often became quite a team of clients but essentially these were to show to Hallet. He performed the essential role of any editor – questioning and challenging, even if the design was almost as desired. He was visually sophisticated and knowledgeable, and their conversation stimulated Pat to refine and complete the image. That relationship became one of the most important in her career (as well as an enduring friendship thriving till her death). Pat's confident and unfailing line combined powerfully with her strict economy with colour, the most elaborate of her designs relying on five colours and an outline, often using clever overprinting and combinations to give the impression of multi-coloured naturalism. The plates shown here are a mixture of designs in gouache and felt pen on watercolour paper (Kent 90lb NOT) and those actually printed on linen or linen union.

Tea towels are ephemeral, even throwaway. Their most everyday of purposes might seem to rob them of any potential dignity. Frayed and holey, hanging on the rail of the Aga or revisited in a pile of ironing, the faded garden of Sissinghurst or ghostly view of Bodiam Castle reappears in ever diminishing focus. But that very quotidian character also makes them familiar – significant even – and most importantly, worthy of the profoundly serious way that their decoration was conceived.

Perhaps the strength of these images comes from this contrast; on one hand Pat's heritage as the child of immigrants from Central Europe, land of peasant art and of simple repeating patterns in bold colours and on the other, the many-stranded

Pat in her studio, 2017.

inheritance of the National Trust, whose custodianship of two great pillars of British culture – the country house and the man-made landscape – represents the very opposite: a complex synergy of high cultural influences.

In the end though these are just the tea towels. Members of the National Trust and visitors to the places it cares for have loved them as much as their creator. Decorative design is at its very best when the designer actually speaks directly to the eventual customer, the consumer, the audience. Pat spoke with a clear voice, stripped of the accents of Mittel Europe or Hull, it was a voice that suited the Trust and that, in a small and specific field, represented all that was best and most remarkable about it.

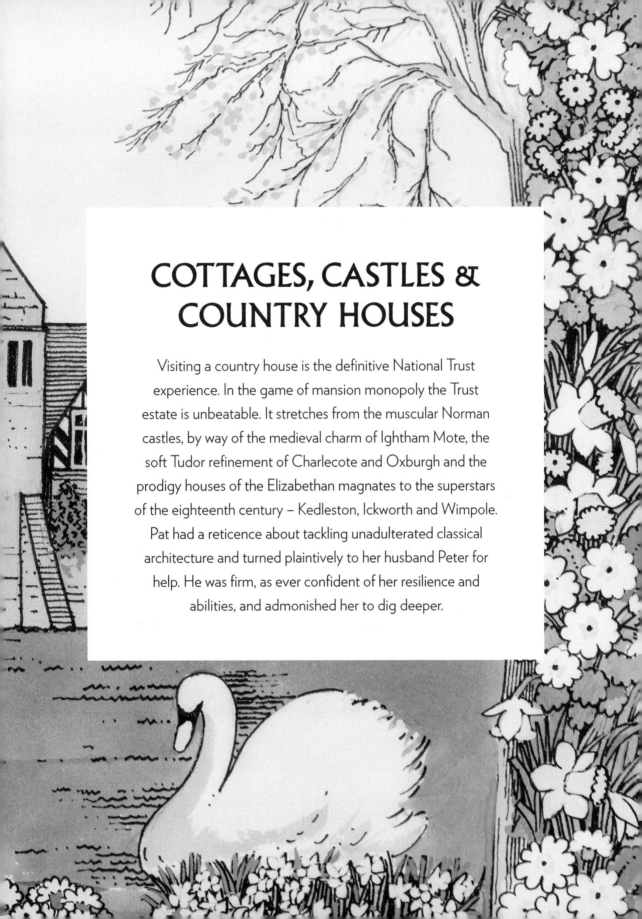

COTTAGES, CASTLES & COUNTRY HOUSES

Visiting a country house is the definitive National Trust experience. In the game of mansion monopoly the Trust estate is unbeatable. It stretches from the muscular Norman castles, by way of the medieval charm of Ightham Mote, the soft Tudor refinement of Charlecote and Oxburgh and the prodigy houses of the Elizabethan magnates to the superstars of the eighteenth century – Kedleston, Ickworth and Wimpole. Pat had a reticence about tackling unadulterated classical architecture and turned plaintively to her husband Peter for help. He was firm, as ever confident of her resilience and abilities, and admonished her to dig deeper.

The colour-washed harling of Scottish castles particularly appealed to Pat and suited her use of flat colour. The grey of the stone roof is used for the unrendered Haddo House in Aberdeenshire.

Designed by Pat Albeck for The National Trust, in conjunction with The William and Mary Tercentenery Trust. IRISH LINEN

1989 marked the tercentenary of the 'Glorious Revolution'. This was the phrase coined for the arrival of William of Orange as husband of Queen Mary and King of England, and the final victory of Protestantism in the country. Bold swags and detailed tulip pots characterise the golden age of English Baroque.

HARDY'S COTTAGE

Thomas Hardy was born here in 1840

MAX GATE

Thomas Hardy designed and lived in this house from 1885 to 1928

'Thomas Hardy'   Designed f   e National Trust by Pat Albeck   IRISH LINEN

14

Pat loved Thomas Hardy. Powerfully romantic with
a highly developed social conscience, he was one of her
literary heroes. He was also important to her editor Ray
Hallet – so a visit to Dorset with him was welcome. They
went to look at the cottage where the author was born
and Max Gate, the house he built himself nearby (he was
originally an architect). These properties are typical of the
kind that are not architecturally significant, but important
because of their associations.

Two Views of Chartwell IRISH LINEN Designed for The National Trust by Pat Albeck

It was typical of Pat's homage to the great wartime leader and his beloved home and retreat at Chartwell in Kent (where he so famously kennelled his black dog horrors with bricklaying and other garden projects) that she should put in pole position Churchill's large ginger tomcat – the other colours in this design take their cue from the cat.

Gladstone's Land. Edinburgh   LINEN   Designed for The National Trust for Scotland by Pat Albeck.

No matter how hard Pat tried to imitate the work of another artist – in this case the painted border on a seventeenth-century ceiling in Edinburgh – it always ended up looking intrinsically hers. Her most deliberate line and natural desire to order and control a pattern always came to the fore.

Designed for The National Trust by Pat Albeck   Irish Linen

Pat was very pleased with these swans but perhaps the design owes more to the beautifully drawn border of primroses and wild daffodil flowers, of which she was very fond.

NYMANS   designed for **THE NATIONAL TRUST** by Pat Albeck   IRISH LINEN

Nymans in West Sussex was twice ruined: once by fire and again in the Great Storm of 1987. Lady Rosse was the last member of the Messel family, who owned the estate, and Pat visited her when staying with her son, Lord Snowdon, nearby. Pat had been a friend of Lady Rosse's brother, the renowned designer Oliver in the 1950s. She designed this towel following the visit.

Pat was most excited to work on this design. Quarry Bank Mill
is a restored eighteenth-century cotton-weaving factory in
Cheshire. The design was the brainchild of Martin Sekers, and
Pat had worked for his father Miki in the 1950s. An émigré
from Hungary, he had established a thriving silk industry
in West Cumberland and was a great supporter of young
designers. So she was most excited to find herself working
with a new generation and produced a group of designs to be
printed on the restored mill machines. The simple flat colours
are reminiscent of eighteenth-century prints.

Lacock in Wiltshire is an extraordinarily beautiful and unspoilt village – in no small part due to the custodianship of the Trust, and before them the Talbot family, who lived at the Abbey. William Fox Talbot was a pioneer of photography and his earliest photographs were taken at Lacock.

Frequently used as a film or television set, Lacock's houses are familiar from many a costume drama. Here they are neatly laid out in schematic form.

A perfect Victorian doll's house frames the calendar months as windows and door, one of the quieter designs of this long series. It is a moot point how many people actually planned their year on linen but this seemed not to adversely affect their decision to buy and to display the tea towels.

THE HOUSEHOLD STAFF Linen Designed by Pat Albeck for The National Trust for Scotland

The house here is Haddo in Aberdeenshire, designed in austere Scottish style by William Adam – but really it is only the background to a group portrait of an imagined household staff. Recent costume dramas have built on a long tradition of below stairs shenanigans, and in this case it has reached the drying-up.

'Hardwick Hall more glass than wall' is a jewel in the Trust's crown, transferred from the glittering coronet of the Duke of Devonshire in lieu of death duties in 1960. Remarkable, as the saying implies, for its impressive use of glass at such an early date but more so as it is a manifestation of the property-enhancing marriages of one powerful sixteenth-century female magnate, Bess of Hardwick. All these things appealed to Pat who was particularly fond of the two tea towels she designed for this Derbyshire property.

Ightham Mote   IRISH LINEN   Designed for The National Trust by Pat Albeck

Ightham Mote in Kent is a relatively recent addition to the Trust, acquired through a legacy in 1985 and not opened until 2004. This design captures the charm of this smaller moated house in bold royal blue and coral with a grisaille vignette of the courtyard in a central lozenge – an unusual format.

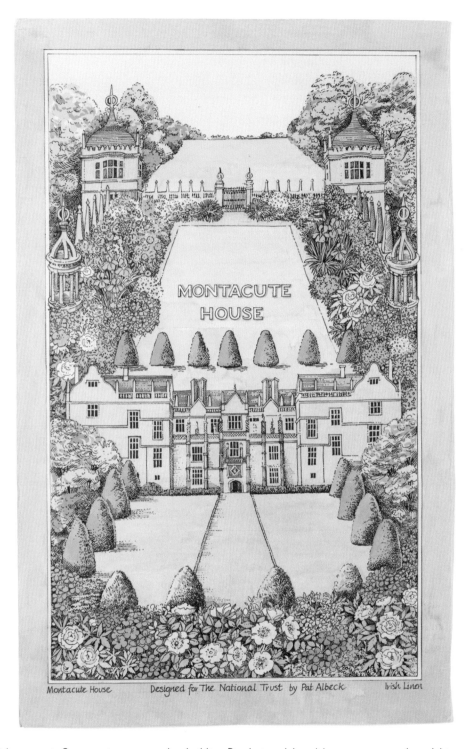

Montacute House   Designed for The National Trust by Pat Albeck   Irish Linen

Montacute in Somerset is an outstanding building. Pat designed three Montacute tea towels, and this is perhaps one of her most assured designs ever. It is a good example of a tea towel in which a simple scheme of five colours and a black outline gives the impression of full colour.

Royal residences was, of course, not designed for the Trust but was one of a group that she produced for the Royal Palaces, indeed one of her last few designs was a cloth for the Prince of Wales' private estate, Highgrove in Gloucestershire. However, it sits comfortably within this collection.

The National Trust in Devon and Cornwall · Pat Albeck

Very early on Pat developed a strong working relationship with Warren Davis, who looked after the West Country administrative region for the Trust and later became press officer for the whole organisation for many years – as well as a close friend. Pat frequently stayed in his cottage at Cotehele in Cornwall.

Some of Pat's early designs were spare and less sophisticated, relying more on drawing and bold colour than elaborate penwork and borders, such as this one depicting Culzean Castle in Ayrshire.

Pat enjoyed a working relationship with the National Trust for Scotland for over 30 years. Her editor there was Elizabeth Renwick, known as Broon.

BRODIE CASTLE   LINEN   Designed for The National Trust for Scotland by Pat Albeck

Not all Pat's property tea towels were produced for the Trust. She worked for many private owners and also for Historic Royal Palaces and Royal Collection. She was the most recognisable and reliable designer to turn to in this small but important field.

BRODICK CASTLE ISLE OF ARRAN   Designed for The National Trust for Scotland by Pat Albeck
LINEN

Pat much enjoyed her Scottish inspiration trips, driving from property to property, drawing and taking photographs (she was an avowedly poor photographer so the drawings were the key). The clear silhouettes of the harled stone castles of the north suited Pat's strong sense of pattern and design and their simplicity allowed deeper concentration on details and pattern in borders.

KITCHENS & FOOD

While polite guides may point out the Gainsborough and the
Lawrence, the ormolu and the satinwood, it is invariably the kitchen
that attracts the crowds. The ranges of copper pans and jelly
moulds and the jumbo chopping boards, the many pantries,
larders and still rooms seem somehow to have an easy resonance.
Pat was no exception, and was always attracted to the scrubbed
kitchen table or the stables. Her taste for the domestic was spiced
up by the visual treats of country house quality and the variety
of her designs was stimulated by these treasure houses. From
the beginning of her career Pat, a passionate, lavish and reliably
delicious cook, had used food as inspiration. The pepper and the
aubergine, the salmon and the lobster – even the sausage was from
time to time pressed into service as a decorative motif.

One of an occasional series of recipe tea towels, the marmalade design was undertaken with huge care and much checking of the actual instructions. Pat was a good preserver – a skill learnt from her long-time housekeeper Mrs Marshall (Maha) rather than from her own mother. Strangely enough marmalade was not her speciality and designing this did not change that.

A more distant but loyal client was the Metropolitan Museum of Art in New York for whom this cloth, inspired by nineteenth-century canning designs, was based. She was especially proud of her work here, perhaps because it looked less like her own.

CREAM TEAS

a recipe for

SCONES

Plain flour	225g	Bi carbonate of soda
Butter	60g	½ level teaspoonful
Milk	150ml	Cream of tartar
Salt ½ teaspoonful		1 level teaspoonful

Sieve flour, bicarbonate of soda, salt & cream of
tartar into a basin, rub in the butter and mix to
a soft dough with the milk. Roll out on a floured
board. The dough should be 12mm thick. Cut into
rounds. Place on a floured baking tray, brush
over with milk and bake in a quick oven
225C (450F gas mark 7) for about 15 minutes.
Serve with cream + strawberry jam

CREAM TEAS   Designed for The National Trust by Pat Albeck   IRISH LINEN

Pat was a cook but not a baker and this design was a
response to a request from the Trust rather than a heartfelt
expression of personal scone-love. It did, however, hit the spot
and was a commercial success, spawning a series of recipe tea
towels over the next decade including a striking marmalade
design (see page 38). They drew a little on a type of French
picture postcard that Pat liked, with lurid photos of
glistening food and a truncated recipe for cassoulet,
Daube de Boeuf or Coquilles St Jacques.

This vegetable rack was Pat's, sitting inside her cottage in Sussex. She was a productive vegetable gardener and this design is particularly personal. Marrows were a loved motif (and she was much given to stuffing them for supper).

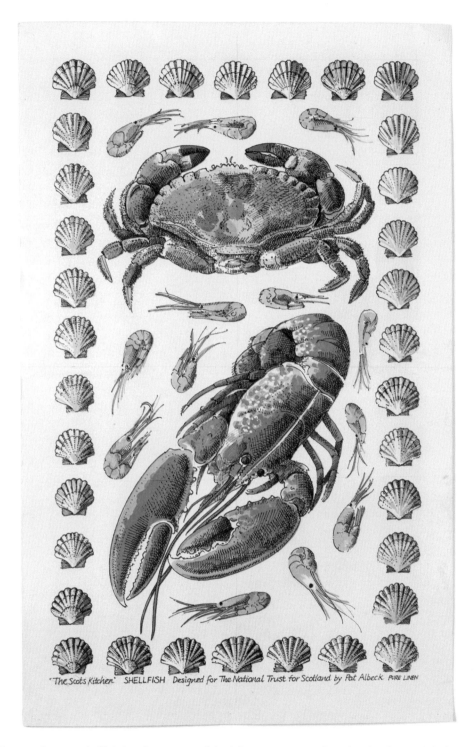

Pat was allergic to shellfish, but she maintained that lobster was exempt from this classification (which occasionally made one doubt the whole ban on Crustacea...). Both they and crabs were good subjects to draw.

'STRAWBERRIES'   PURE LINEN   Designed for The National Trust for Scotland by Pat Albeck

During the Second World War two of Pats sisters, Sheila and Gwen, were land girls in East Yorkshire. Pat longed to be asked to help but was firmly rebuffed as too small (she was born in 1930). In particular she wanted to pick strawberries and this came up repeatedly when, later in life, she would enthusiastically visit various pick-your-own fruit farms. So the romance of this strawberry cloth is particularly significant.

'Table lay thyself' was an idea that pleased Pat, and a lavish feast gave her great (visual) pleasure. Austerity had little appeal – in design or in life – perhaps a response to wartime rationing.

The Kitchen at Lanhydrock IRISH LINEN Designed for The National Trust by Pat Albeck

This was Pat's favourite design. These tessellating jelly moulds, copper pans and rolling pins were in the kitchen at Lanhydrock. The stroke of visual genius that displayed them on a hot blue background sings strikingly with the orange-y browns and is one of the most graphically striking of all her towels; its strength derived from a combination of careful, detailed drawing, with utter simplicity of conception and design.

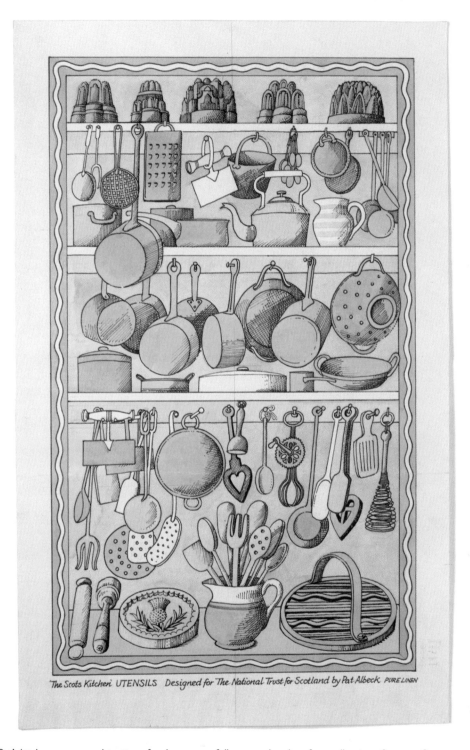

'The Scots Kitchen' UTENSILS Designed for The National Trust for Scotland by Pat Albeck PURE LINEN

Pat's kitchen was a combination of order – a carefully curated and profuse collection of pottery from Clarice Cliff to eighteenth-century Wedgwood – and the utter chaos of somebody for whom washing up was one task too many. This tidy dresser is redolent of many a 1970s country kitchen.

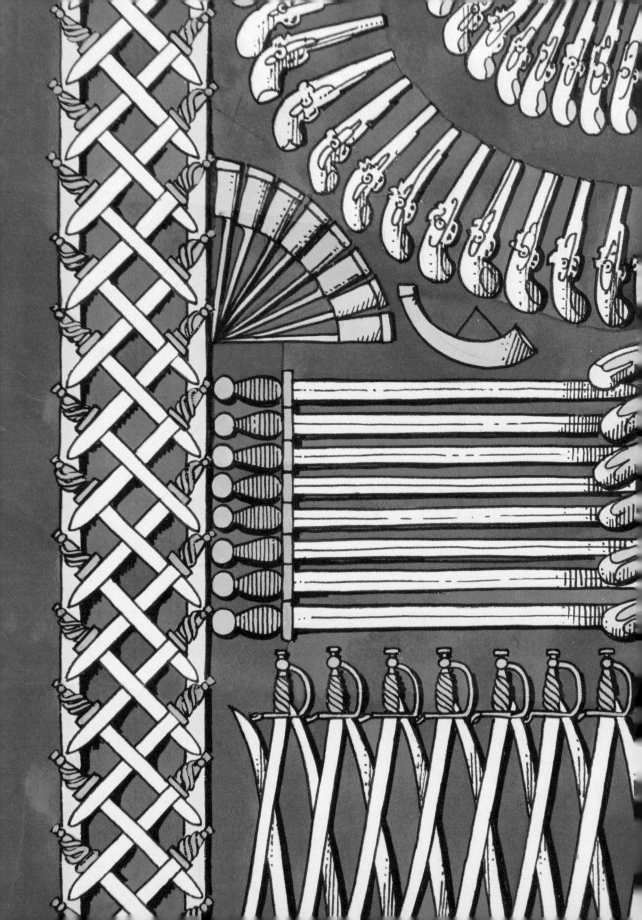

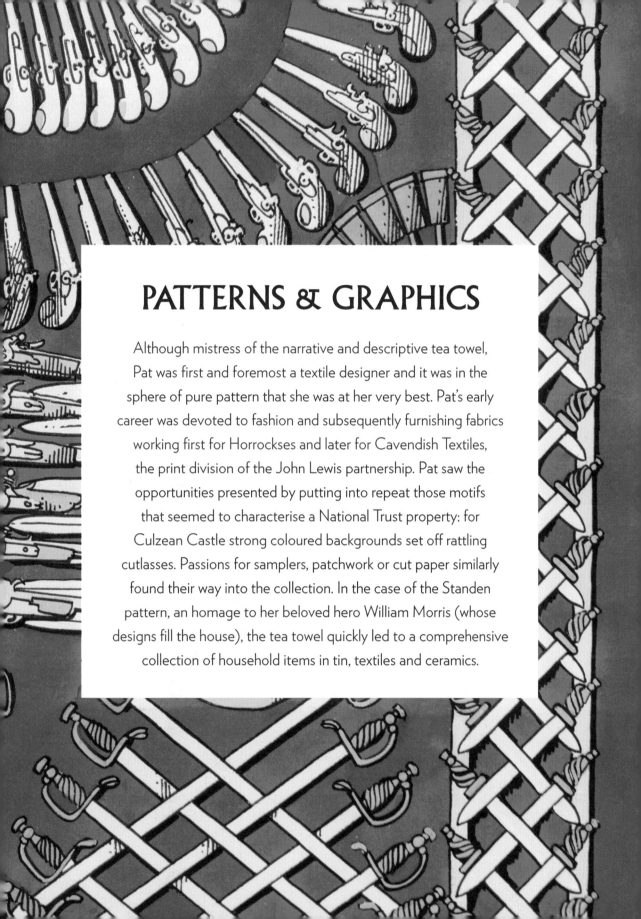

PATTERNS & GRAPHICS

Although mistress of the narrative and descriptive tea towel,
Pat was first and foremost a textile designer and it was in the
sphere of pure pattern that she was at her very best. Pat's early
career was devoted to fashion and subsequently furnishing fabrics
working first for Horrockses and later for Cavendish Textiles,
the print division of the John Lewis partnership. Pat saw the
opportunities presented by putting into repeat those motifs
that seemed to characterise a National Trust property: for
Culzean Castle strong coloured backgrounds set off rattling
cutlasses. Passions for samplers, patchwork or cut paper similarly
found their way into the collection. In the case of the Standen
pattern, an homage to her beloved hero William Morris (whose
designs fill the house), the tea towel quickly led to a comprehensive
collection of household items in tin, textiles and ceramics.

'Birds and Fruit' IRISH LINEN Designed for The National Trust by Pat Albeck

Sometimes Pat experimented with new techniques. She was most excited by this woodcut/linocut approach and it certainly uses the printing limitations to remarkable and new effect.

The bleached timber studding and colour-washed infill of Lavenham's medieval houses are of great interest to lovers of old buildings but for Pat they became an arrangement of vertical stripes and triangles. She was pleased to note that they were reminiscent of her parents' half-timbered 1930s villa in Hull.

Pat's ornithological interests were severely limited –
although fond of chickens and more so of white ducks –
blackbirds were really the only wild bird she claimed an
interest in (actually she also liked song thrushes...), perhaps
because with their untroubled black outfits and smart yellow
beaks they were a strong contrast with a flowery background,
as this design shows so well. The jewel-like tapestry of wild
flowers was a trope to which she repeatedly returned.

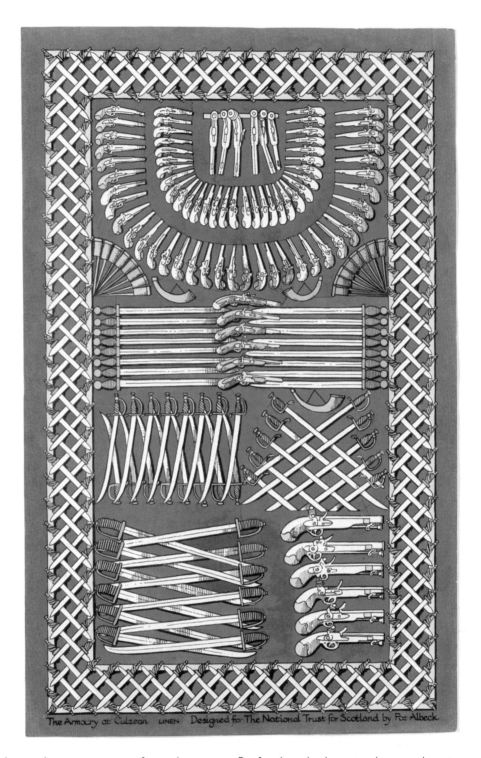

The Armoury at Culzean LINEN Designed for The National Trust for Scotland by Pat Albeck

Arms and armour were never of particular interest to Pat, for whom the domestic sphere was always in the ascendancy. But the patterns into which these were arranged at Culzean Castle in Ayrshire definitely did attract her attention.

'Treasures from 'The Mary Rose'   Designed by Pat Albeck for The Mary Rose Museum

As late as 2015 Pat much enjoyed her visit to the restored wreck of the *Mary Rose*, unusually for her in a wheelchair kindly pushed around the museum by its chairman Admiral John Lippiett. 'Very good looking,' she commented, before producing this splendid design based on the treasures rescued when the ship was raised from the sea floor 20 years earlier. At 85 she was still at the height of her powers.

Standen   IRISH LINEN   Designed for The National Trust by Pat Albeck

William Morris, designer, entrepreneur and socialist, was Pat's particular hero. The bearded giant of the Victorian decorative arts was much admired by Pat's adored father and this design was in the spirit of a humble acolyte (not a frequently assumed persona for Pat, who was an utterly confident designer). Morris, while a sophisticated and sinuous twister and manipulator of the natural world, was also a faithful portraitist of his floral models, capturing their particular form and growth even in the most highly wrought design. Pat was channelling Morris' popular print 'Strawberry Thief' when she was producing 'Standen' but somehow the line and colour and eventually the whole design becomes her own.

ORANGE TREE   Designed for The National Trust by Pat Albeck   IRISH LINEN

Part-stained glass but perhaps just a straightforwardly decorative design of the sort that came very directly from Pat's designer's mind: flat colour, repeating borders of a basically floral theme, a controlled palette of bright, non-primary colours and a clear message.

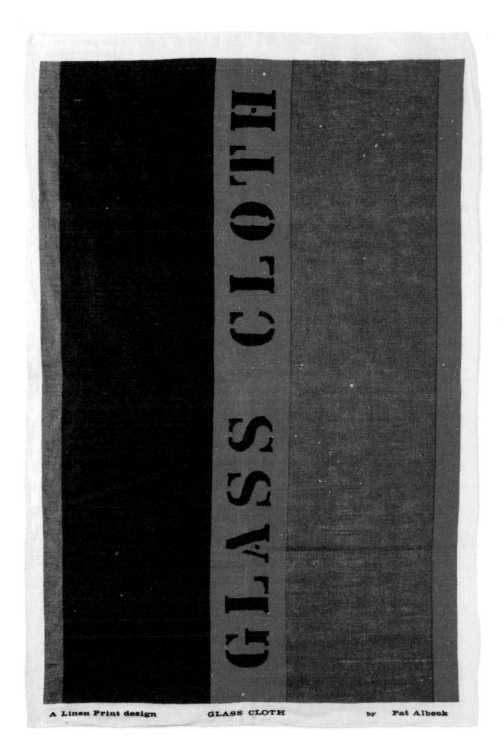

This uncharacteristically spare design, printed linen in imitation of a woven cloth, is a design from the 1950s produced for Cavendish Textiles. It was a great favourite, and Pat felt it needed no more embellishment.

The endless boredom of a Victorian childhood had some
dividends and the long afternoons of ennui gave rise to
the sampler, a demonstration of a young girl's virtuoso skill
with needle and embroidery thread. Familiar symbols – house,
flower, leaf or crown – decorated an alphabet or thoughtful
motto, all on a cream linen ground, such as the example seen
here inspired by the sampler collection at Montacute. They
appealed to Pat, who revisited them several times – once
as the theme for one of over 40 National Trust calendar tea
towels that she produced (the first in 1976, the last for 2019).

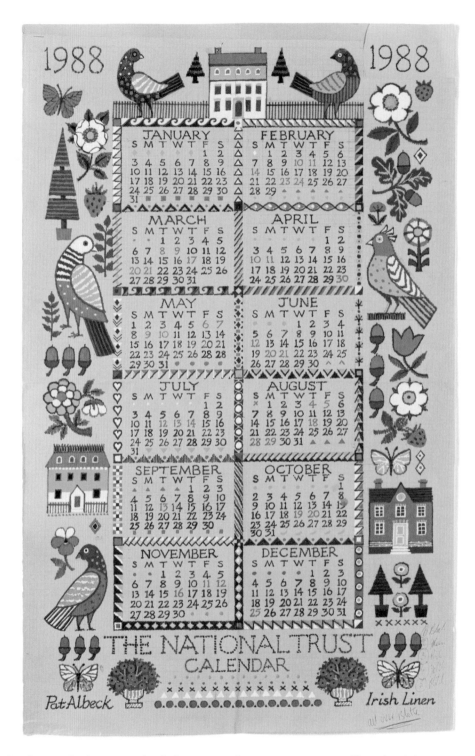

Another sampler, this time used to find a new way of representing a property. The isolated elements are also inspired by sixteenth- and seventeenth-century stumpwork embroidery.

Pat never made a patchwork although she was for a time an inspired designer and executor of petit point embroidery... but the tumbling dice motif seen here was one that gave her great pleasure.

Fast colours

Jonelle

All pure linen

Pat produced this series of cloths for Jonelle, part of the John Lewis Partnership, in the 1950s. They were in uncompromisingly bold colours and the stark arrangement of symbols on a plain white ground is striking. She carried out these designs in cut paper and tissue paper, a style to which she was to return half a century later.

All pure linen   Jonelle   Fast colours

These three almost bilious green fish are quite fat, as were most of Pat's animals. While the designs are formalised – almost iconographic – they are still clearly fish with the correct number and disposition of fins.

BACK TO THE GARDEN

A design for a particularly stylish organic farm shop in Norfolk belonging to her friend the actor and landowner Delaval Astley. They were both members of a poetry group, and she very much loved his voice and delivery. Cut paper again...

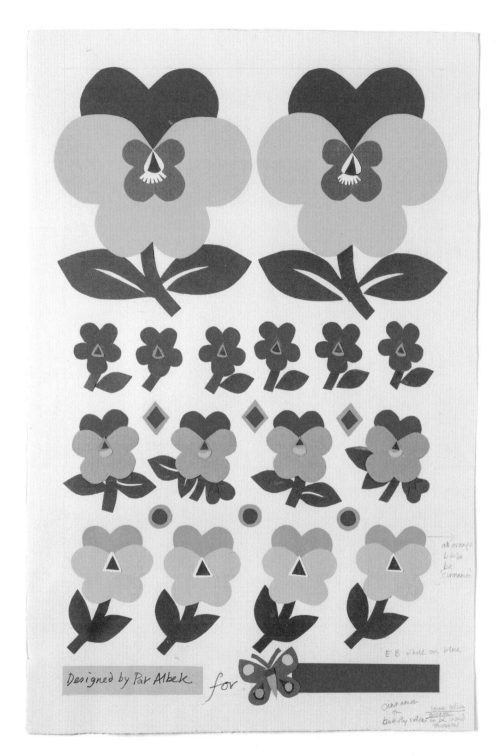

Designed by Pat Albeck for

Pat would buy pansies with minimum provocation. A large earthenware pot of them was often found beside her front door, despite her husband Peter's 65-year, much-voiced resistance to their charms. She was much taken with the seemingly endless variations that breeders could evolve into and the simple, face-like geometry of their smiling flowers.

CAROLINE

CAROLINE

designed for The National Trust by Pat Albeck

Caroline was one of several doll tea towels designed to be cut out and sewn into real dolls. The ensuing doll or girl was rather long and thin but otherwise she would have looked huge when flat.

Chickens were often used as inspiration and a small flock lived in the back of Pat's London garden in the days before the feral foxes that appeared in the garden made this seem impossible. The lacing of their feathers (where one coloured feather is lined with another) appealed to her desire for pattern in all things.

Pat's pleasure in manipulating lettering is attested to by its
frequent use in her designs. This second design for Quarry
Bank Mill is just such a cloth (incidentally, printed on cotton
not linen as this was what was actually woven in that rural
Cheshire factory). With the writing in strong diagonals and
in varying decorated and open face fonts, the pattern has
something of the nineteenth-century trade advertisement
about it. The National Trust acorn, seen through the prism of
Victorian prints, is woven amongst the lettering and the design
is printed in two screens only adding to its engraved quality.

BIRDS & BEASTS

In truth Pat was not an animal person although a devoted owner of a string of five labradors. Her passion was cats. It was with the greatest difficulty that she was restrained from bringing back a succession of kittens and cats from every holiday. She recalled with surprising accuracy a tabby from Naxos, a pale pastel ginger from Venice or a particularly neatly marked black and white specimen from the south of France. Jolly, her white cat, was a frequently recurring subject. But her models were not all to be found at home and knowing her audience well, she produced a series of National Trust cats tea towels, each featuring a group of feline portraits of the house cats of varying properties. Dogs followed. With other animals she had been known to ask her husband or son to provide a frog, heron, or otter...

BIRDS AT BROWNSEA ISLAND   designed for The National Trust by Pat Albeck

Pat once said that until she became the mother of a bird-mad son she just thought there were robins, blackbirds and then other birds that looked only slightly different – the entire world of classification, families and species had passed her by. But the use of pattern in God's creation resonated with her and it is no surprise that she favoured those birds with strong graphic credentials.

The unicorn tapestries at the Metropolitan Museum of New York's medieval outpost, The Cloisters, were a major source of inspiration for Pat; the jewel-like detail and botanical accuracy were easily transferable to Pat's sharp pen and brush. The museum was a good client and an excuse to visit Manhattan.

CAT ON A PAISLEY SHAWL. IRISH LINEN. Designed for The National Trust for Scotland by Pat Albeck

There are certain design symbols that recur year
after year and the paisley is just such a shape and style.
The easily recognised curled teardrop, while first
associated with a small Scottish industrial town of the
same name, is in fact originally derived from Indian
textiles. The white cat is the designer's own.

Pollyanna

from POWIS CASTLE

There were two versions of this design. The idea was strong and resonated especially well with regular visitors, who grew to know the feline guards and residents of their favourite property. However, even well-protected National Trust cats do, from time to time, move on to the heavenly mousing grounds, and new characters arrive to take their place necessitating a revision of this tea towel. From time to time a new cat would retain the name of its predecessor (and theirs before them) providing editorial confusion. Although some cats were recorded face to face, others were sent to Pat as photographs, and many more than could ever be included. Awkward decisions had to be made...

The success of National Trust cats (and indeed Canterbury Cathedral cats) crossed species to a selection of canine Trust supporters.

The Home Farm, Wimpole.   IRISH LINEN   Designed for The National Trust by Pat Albeck

Wimpole outside Cambridge is a much-visited Trust property, but as well as the Hardwicke family's splendid mansion and extensive park, it has a splendid model farm designed by Sir John Soane in 1794. This design softens the austere, mannered architecture with charming animal portraits.

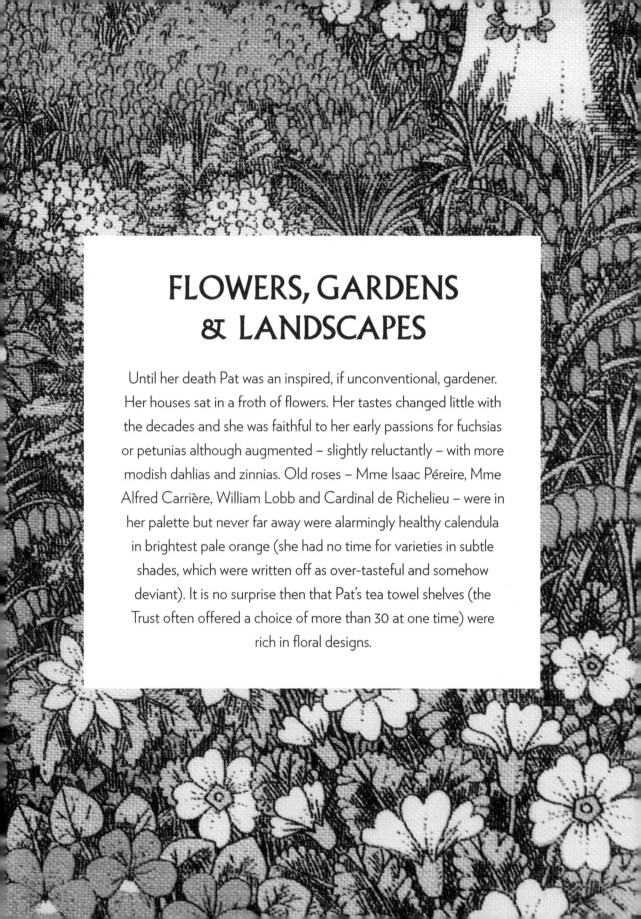

FLOWERS, GARDENS & LANDSCAPES

Until her death Pat was an inspired, if unconventional, gardener. Her houses sat in a froth of flowers. Her tastes changed little with the decades and she was faithful to her early passions for fuchsias or petunias although augmented – slightly reluctantly – with more modish dahlias and zinnias. Old roses – Mme Isaac Péreire, Mme Alfred Carrière, William Lobb and Cardinal de Richelieu – were in her palette but never far away were alarmingly healthy calendula in brightest pale orange (she had no time for varieties in subtle shades, which were written off as over-tasteful and somehow deviant). It is no surprise then that Pat's tea towel shelves (the Trust often offered a choice of more than 30 at one time) were rich in floral designs.

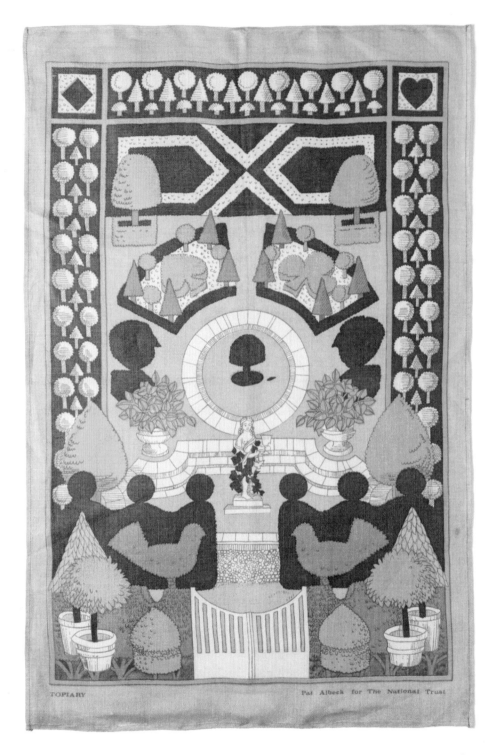

Topiary, being all green, is ideal for a limited palette and allows for the use of several shades, making for a highly decorative design with yew and box and near parterres.

Designed by Pat Albeck for The National Trust for Scotland   PURE LINEN

From time to time the Trust has an annual focus – Enterprise Neptune, for example, was a coastline year – and this cloth was made to celebrate National Trust gardens. Topiary writing was a solution Pat liked and it works well here.

A Present from
The National Trust

Irish Linen

Pat Albeck

There was a particular 1950s passion for Victoriana, and Pat
and Peter subscribed to this true faith, whose high priests
were John Betjeman, John Piper and Laurence Scarfe,
publisher of the much-fêted *Saturday Book*, a series of albums
of decorative miscellanies that continued until the 1970s. It
particularly favoured those artefacts that were at the same
time sentimental but beautifully drawn. Staffordshire figures,
sailor's valentines, Sunderland Lustreware and other decorative
oddities all pleased the neo-Romantics. Pat's invented mug 'A
present from The National Trust' comes from the same cultural
stable. Here it is stuffed with a colourful bunch of wild flowers,
again appealing to that aesthetic. It was a bestseller...

Lettering is powerful. Everybody understands it and each shape is familiar. The jigsaw challenge of arranging the individual characters so that they also read as a word was one that Pat returned throughout her career. This cloth sat well alongside several others in what was her favourite palette in the late 1970s.

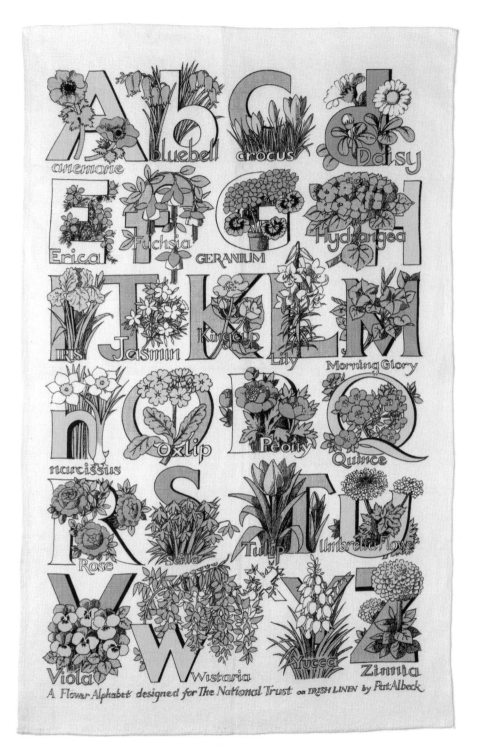

A Flower Alphabet designed for The National Trust on IRISH LINEN by Pat Albeck

A decorative alphabet is a design solution that allows 26 details to be brought into play. Here they represent different facets of the work of the National Trust. Designs like this were particularly useful as they could be sold in any one of the 300 National Trust shops.

'Kitchen Garden' Designed for The National Trust on Irish Linen by Pat Albeck

The kitchen garden summed up all that was best for Pat – a synergy of food, summer and gardening. Over the years Pat had several gardens of her own, including a much-loved loan of a crumbling greenhouse belonging to adored friends and neighbours in Norfolk. She would drive the three miles to their walled garden and with tiny fork, spade and rake magic up a Tuscan market full of produce.

The Rose + Iris Garden

The White Garden

The Lily Garden

The Vegetable Garden

Barrington Court Gardens   Designed for The National Trust by Pat Albeck   IRISH LINEN

The great joy of a wall lined with fruit trees and neat rows of crops was a weed-free and utterly pleasurable dream for Pat, as was a tidy potting shed. It fuelled many designs like this and was a recurring theme in her work. Though energetic in the garden, she never achieved such geometric accuracy.

'MECONOPSIS' Designed for The National Trust for Scotland on pure linen by Pat Albeck

It was a source of much regret that in nearly 60 years of gardening Pat never grew Meconopsis poppies. Californian, Iceland, oriental... even one called 'Patty's plum' were her reliable subjects, but never the elusive pure blue holy grail. So she made good that gap with a full-blooded drift of them in this tea towel.

SPRINGTIME   Irish Linen   Designed for The National Trust by Pat Albeck

Pat saw the landscape in detail and the overview was never important. Here she struggled to combine a patchwork carpet of woodland-floor flowers with tree trunks. The scale issues this threw up were challenging and yet the synthesis does still work.

HYDRANGEAS   IRISH LINEN   Designed for The National Trust by Pat Albeck

94

Pat and Peter rented a cottage in Sussex for over 20 years
and had much fun filling it with Victorian furniture and
ceramics bought in local junk shops. One, now long gone,
in Westbourne yielded an especially rich harvest, including
this large jug – in fact a pitcher – and ewer bedroom set.
Decorated with faded clover leaves it stood on a staircase
windowsill and was filled every year with hydrangeas
throughout the autumn and winter.

THE WHITE GARDEN · SISSINGHURST   IRISH LINEN   Designed for The National Trust by Pat Albeck.

The famous white garden at Sissinghurst, Kent, was one of many important gardens that were tackled in Pat's lifetime of designing. Pat's visual sympathies and tastes probably lay more with the gardens of Vita Sackville West's granddaughter-in-law Sarah Raven but she knew a good thing when she saw it and much enjoyed her visit and tea with Nigel Nicolson (Vita's son) after drawing the garden.

Back to The Cloisters in Upper Manhattan. This reconstruction of French medieval building transported across the Atlantic has been part of the Metropolitan Museum of Art in New York since 1934. The extraordinary juxtaposition of eighth-century France and Fort Tyron Park next to the Hudson River was as amazing to Pat as to its millions of visitors and she was exceptionally proud of this design.

Giant's Causeway in Northern Ireland is a very important part of the National Trust, and is its most visited site. The tessellating hexagons, so unlikely in nature, appealed to Pat and the landmark featured in her designs more than once.

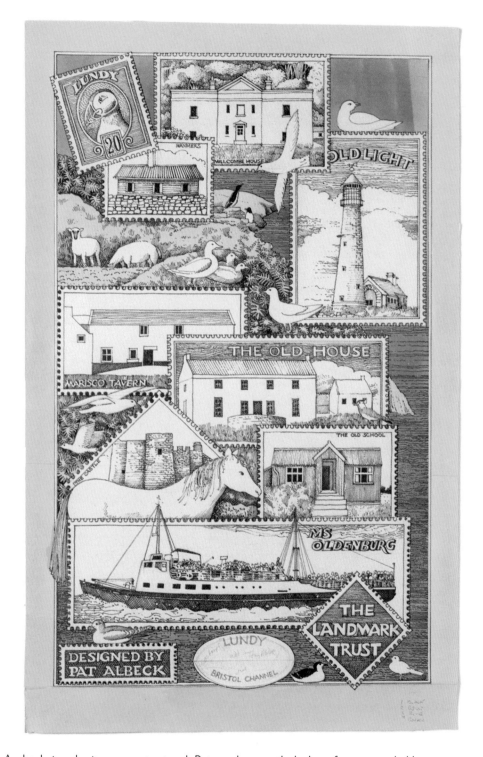

As she designed quite so many tea towels Pat was always on the look out for a new angle. Here the seaside postcard (not the rosy bottom and hanky-covered head variety) provided a new form to work with.

Roses at Mottisfont   *Designed for The National Trust by Pat Albeck*

Old roses had much significance for Pat. She was of the generation that rediscovered these subtle and refined variations of pinkness and rejected the slightly veg-like energy of the hybrid tea. So the Trust's gardens at Mottisfont, Hampshire, were significant. The roses here are mixed with spires of white foxgloves.

THE NATIONAL TRUST

Ash

Cedar

Elm

Lime

Sycamore

Holly

Yew

Chestnut

Beech

Hawthorn

Oak

Irish Linen

TREES

Designed by Pat Albeck

A spare design of trees. With the exception of Gerard Manley Hopkins' cherry tree, the world of trunk and branch and silhouetted foliage meant little to Pat, for whom they were really green cauliflowers on sticks. Nevertheless she could turn her workmanlike hand to most subjects and here they are given the treatment.

Watersmeet in Devon was a favourite design. Pat was pleased with the white border, the woodland flower frame and the treatment of the waterfalls. Perhaps it was also a good day out, maybe with a delicious pub lunch with Ray Hallet that made this an oft-referred to tea towel.

CASTLE DROGO GARDENS   Designed for The National Trust by Pat Albeck   IRISH LINEN

For a building this beefy and robust, Edwin Lutyens' western masterpiece Castle Drogo, Devon, is given the smallest role to play in this design that makes more of the gardens than the house itself. The chequerboard planting makes a strong pattern at the centre of the cloth, as does the bold green border.

FUSCHIA   IRISH LINEN   Designed for The National Trust by Pat Albeck

Pat, though utterly cognisant of all nuances of good taste in home and garden and thoroughly exposed to the slightest changes in such orthodoxies, could and did break out. A recurring example of this was her undimmable passion for fuchsias. These frequently lurid pink and purple constructions always incurred a pursing of the lips from refined gardeners but to Pat they were pure glamour.

Flower Show   The National Trust   Irish Linen

The geranium in bold cadmium red or aniline pink, Senetti and even the African violet are greenhouse plants that had been unfashionable since the 1930s, but Pat held a candle for these strong growing, brightly coloured troopers – and indeed her doorway was never without a few pots of them (she did draw the line at hanging baskets but could probably have been persuaded...).

WILD FLOWERS   IRISH LINEN   Designed for The National Trust by Pat Albeck

The terrific richness of wild flowers was a total pleasure to Pat, and with its refined and accurate illustration Rev. Keble Martin's colour-coded *The Concise British Flora in Colour* was her bible. Many of those favourite subjects are combined in this design, which spread into countless other household products.

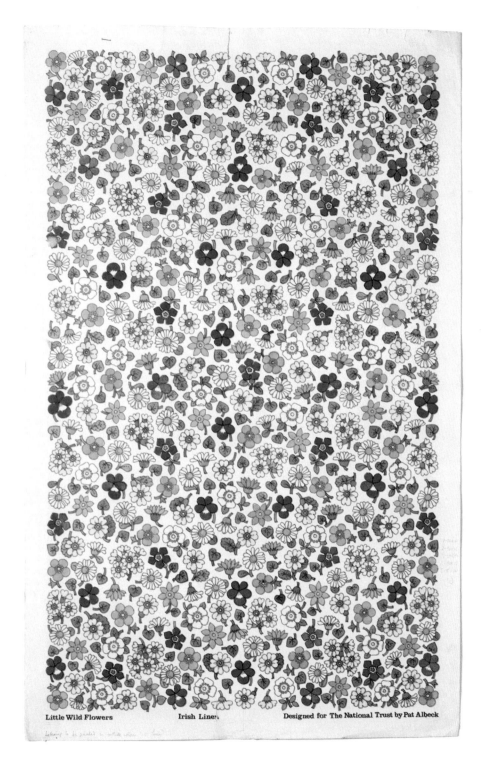

Little Wild Flowers   Irish Linen   Designed for The National Trust by Pat Albeck

A tighter and richer wild flower meadow appears in one of Pat's trademark almost invisible repeats. This was a commercial success for the National Trust for many years.

ICKWORTH   IRISH LINEN   Designed for The National Trust by Pat Albeck

Ickworth in Suffolk is a most peculiar classical confection of the Marquesses of Bristol, and its story has been a chequered one to say the least. When drawing this Pat stayed with her former secretary Tangy Heron who, most implausibly, managed to get her mounted on quite a large horse. This was so much more extraordinary than Ickworth itself that, for her, it forever overshadowed this design.

Pat was every bit as devoted to the National Trust for Scotland as to the National Trust (and also to its commercial director Micky Blacklock who she loved). The Scottish designs number among her very best, and this lush, abundant towering basket of flowers is just one such tour de force.

Pat's first calendar tea towel was destined to serve for the year of that searingly hot summer, so perhaps the bleached dried-grass colour of the background was prescient. Even after the National Trust turned their back on the tea towel the linen calendar proved too popular to abandon and Pat provided designs for 43 consecutive years.

Pat died with resolute calm and decisive dignity in September 2017, a year after her beloved husband Peter. They were both 87. Two lives well-lived and loved were marked by obituaries in all the broadsheets, and in Pat's case a further obituary on BBC Radio 4 (following on from her appearance on *Desert Island Discs*, broadcast in 2015). She was working until three days before her death and, a week before that, rolled up, wrapped around a tube and sent to the National Trust, her last tea towel. It is not her most important, perhaps not her best ever but it was the utterly professional signing-off of an undiminished career of nearly 70 years. She left behind an extraordinary legacy of work, collected, loved and studied. She lived long enough to enjoy the social media for which she and her work were ideally suited. This book shows just a small section of that oeuvre stretching from fashion and furnishing to books (she wrote several for grown-ups, children and an excellent text book for students). Despite the intrinsic funniness of designing hundreds of tea towels, it is a part of her career about which she was in deadly earnest, and so they are a good and representative illustration of a life spent designing. She would be very pleased to be showing them to you.

Matthew, her son
2018

INDEX

Page numbers in *italics*
refer to illustrations